LOST IN STATIC

LOST IN STATIC

Selected Digital Poems: 2019-2023

Samira Vivette

Lost in Static: Selected Digital Poems 2019-2023

ISBN: 978-0-6451638-7-2

Join me on this pixelated journey
of words originally shared
and read on the screen.

LOST IN STATIC

Now is finally time to run toward what is mine, imagination flowing freely, heart bursting with a special kind of magic, knowing this suffering was the stepping stone to new beginnings.

If I lose my willingness to trust people after mine was broken, they win. From that moment on, I will be robbed of all future opportunities that require vulnerability and openness. By keeping my guard up a little too high, I won't witness the gift of somebody relating to a wound of mine, helping each other move forward toward the light. By allowing those who broke my trust to continue on while I carry their baggage, I am the one who suffers. I don't want to live in fear of something as beautiful and powerful as a genuine connection. I won't let them hurt me again after they're gone. I won't give them that kind of power.

When I speak about knowing my worth, it's not coming from a place of ego or arrogance. I stand by my positive attributes with conviction but the difference is I'm conscious of my shortfalls and work on them every day. When somebody holds a space in my heart, there is nothing I wouldn't do for them. Generosity, patience, and loyalty are traits of mine cherished dearly by those who know me. But I won't pretend other emotions don't consume me. Because they do. However, it is my unwavering devotion to give the positivity inside me a stronger voice – one which overrides all. When I say I know my worth, it's because I've done the work to get here. It's because I continue doing so. I know what I have to offer. And I stand strong in that fact alone.

I am letting go and trusting what's mine will make its way home. I set free any resistance between what I think I want and what is meant for me. If my past up until now is any indication as to how my life will turn out, I am grateful for everything. I am still here, and I am still learning. The lessons, the memories, the heartbreak – I am accepting it all with open arms. I am trusting the Universe is guiding me toward my destiny, toward my home.

Sometimes,
it's not even worth
opening your mouth
to explain your story
to those who were too quick
to take another side.

This is where I retreat,
wish them well,
and leave them behind
with a smile.

I gravitate toward like-minded spirits who are willing to shake the ground and embrace their character. I am intrigued by difference, resistance, brokenness, and disaster.

The world needs more emotional vulnerability. The world needs more transparency. The world needs more people being honest about how they feel. The world needs less ego, less fear, less living according to others' opinions. The ideals of radical self-love and cherishing others intensely are not mutually exclusive. You can do both. You should do both. You can miss and appreciate connections and acknowledge the impact somebody has made in your life while also respecting yourself and investing in your growth. Many live in fear of honesty by portraying an unbothered front due to being hurt in the past or giving too much weight to external perceptions of them. But when I see somebody in tune with their emotions, all I see is a soul housing an abundance of strength, self-awareness, and radiance–because this is a person who has been through too much pain, too much loss, and does not have a second left to waste being somebody they're not.

Those who are threatened by your progress will try to knock you down a peg and bet on the hope you loathe yourself enough to listen to them.

Change nothing. If anything, fight even harder.

Your greatest power is persisting regardless.

And I hope on those mornings your body hurts to move and your spirit wishes to stay still, you find your energy in the little things around you that keep your heart full.

Only you know who you are and how far you've come. Take up space. Embrace your flaws. Forgive yourself for your mistakes. Continue on this road with self-assurance because you are moving in the right direction, even if it doesn't feel like it. Everything is lining up for you. The right opportunities are coming your way. The right people will always stay. You haven't undergone this agonizing growth in vain. Blessings are on the horizon.

May you feel the power
that emerges after the
seemingly helpless
find their purpose.

I often think about everything that has led me to the present moment. No mistakes were made. There are no doubts to be had. Every time the debris of a choice or lack thereof shook me to my core, it was only a matter of time before the Universe revealed *the why*. It was only a matter of time before contentment became the overruling essence in my heart and mind. Regret ensues when suffering accompanies reflection. Regrets occur when somebody looks back on their life and believes every action has contributed to their misfortune. And some people endure a greater degree of torment than others. This is undeniable. But I do believe that sometimes the crumbling enables the creation of a foundation more aligned with our purpose. I believe the devastation is there to also teach us a lesson: to help us find our purpose, to remind us of our strength, to gift us the resilience to build ourselves up from nothing once more while finding solace in the constellations within our spirits, far beyond our physical bodies.

Radiate truth and honesty with a hint of darkness and mystery.

The mind is the most powerful thing. You master that, you master anything. Nobody knows you better than you know yourself. In this world, your skeleton is the only thing you can carry with conviction. Others' opinions will get under your skin and fight for permanent residency, but you have the power to choose what makes it past the doors and what drowns in the moat. There will be intent to weaken the ideologies that keep you bound together, that keep you solidly upright. But anything meant to destroy your castle will prove futile because even if it shakes, even if it trembles, your foundation at its core remains unbreakable. There may be rocks thrown trying to bring down your home, but what they will never know is these doubts about your character have been lived and trialed until ego and self-assurance have seeped from its walls. So, stand tall against them all. They can't make it past your gates because nobody, fucking nobody gets to tell you who you are and who you aren't if they haven't lived a day in your place.

This clear conscience is worth
every single grain of suffering.
I may have been collateral damage,
but I learn from my tribulations
and always come back stronger.
I know the person I am.
And I know my intentions.

I hope you understand that, darling.

My patience and understanding are innate traits I would never change for anything.

But my devoted nature is not to be mistaken for gullibility.

I can just as easily disconnect at the first sign of disrespect.
I won't allow anyone to treat me less than I deserve again.

Appreciate the kind ones. Hold them dearly. Show them their light is seen. Give them justice in this world to let them know their character is valued above all. It is these souls who have been taken advantage of the most – and the heartbreaking truth is less and less remain after the remainder turn cold. Cherish them. Give them hope. Allow them to be comfortable in a place where they are not the norm because they deserve nothing but eternal warmth.

With every suppressed emotion awaits distress on the other end of the spectrum. Regret weighs heavier than embarrassment.

I adore my flaws with the same intensity as my strengths. Admittance of my imperfections and acceptance of who I am has brought me more peace than trying to hide or change them. And this does not involve the deficits which can be improved such as disadvantageous coping mechanisms or the way I react in certain situations meant to trigger me. I mean the awkwardly vibrant facets of my personality that were neglected externally and must be nourished by me and only me. I welcome them wholeheartedly. I have set aside a space for them to just… be.

I would always find parts of myself in those I fell for and feel an overwhelming sense of loss when our connection died.

But then I realized the very thing I missed was a reflection of my magic and it wasn't theirs to keep.

This wonderment was always mine to take back, to carry home with me.

The belief cherished
within myself
holds more weight
than their pessimistic
projections.

I will lose everyone
and everything
before I lose myself
again.

To live in a shell
made from the
validation of others
at your expense
is an exhausting,
soul-destroying
existence that
makes you wish
you were dead.

After unlocking my full potential, discarding the projections, achieving goal after goal, and excelling in those aspects of my life I once called a dream, I now know with certainty the ones who tried to keep me down saw something special in me from the beginning.

But instead of choosing support, genuine energy, and being by each other's sides on this journey to succeed, they made the choice to be the ones to watch me.

The tables always turn.

Make sure you're at peace
with the side you chose.

And when you finally put your foot down, ensure it is done with conviction because they turned a blind eye to your suffering and will continue to until you show them your integrity isn't for the taking.

Mess up.
Learn from your mistakes.
Indulge in the madness.
Do it all again.

Be as gentle as the breeze
and as rough as the storm.

Seek solace in the stars.
Embrace the light
and the dark.

But never apologize
for who you are.

Allow yourself the same compassion extended to others on those days when mistakes and lapses of judgment are plentiful. Acknowledge your imperfections as a human being and their cruciality in paving the way for acceptance, spiritual nourishment, and delving deeper into your healing. You will eventually find complete contentment in the person you are, although this journey may take time: embrace each and every facet of your soul and unlearn the fear of being vulnerable. You have spent a lifetime growing into your skin. You know who you are beneath it all regardless of what they think. Now is the time to shed the ideologies that left you in ruins. This is the final phase of evolution where you definitively turn inward.

I have yet to wake up
and experience a day
without making a list.
And I think that says
everything
it needs to
about the way
us humans
exist.

The skill of self-reflection is an important one to practice because we are not always right and there is forever room to grow. Sometimes, certain encounters hit a nerve and trigger what may seem like an overreaction. Each person has undergone different experiences, and to deny bias in decision-making is unrealistic. But the ideal of growth includes approaching life moving forward with a streak of open-mindedness. We are entitled to feel overwhelmed, doubtful, and offended in some situations. And we may be valid in our responses according to our individual perspective. However, searching for the reason it managed to get under our skin is important. Acknowledging a conflicting point of view, although it may not align with ours, is crucial to one's evolution. Admitting our mistakes is important. Finding our voice is important. Forgiving ourselves for our imperfect existence is crucial. And seeking improvement where possible should be non-negotiable. But we won't always get it right and please everybody on this journey. All we can do it try to see life from other angles and make active efforts to learn in every situation.

I can never hold
one speck of animosity
toward those I loved
and who loved me
who grew distant to
find their own path
on life's journey.

Beautiful souls
deserve the world,
even if we don't end
up in it together.

They can speak about how they would have done things differently, but they weren't in your place to make that decision.

Make peace with it.

You did what you thought was right at the time.

You can say
you deserve good things
for years and years
and feel nothing.

But one day,
it will click.

Those words
won't feel so empty.
The syllables will course
through you like electricity.
You'll feel a neglected part
of your soul that you didn't
know could ache with hope
come out of the woodwork.

That is the day
your worthiness
will make itself known.

There's a deep sadness within me that accumulates when things change. The inevitability of losing touch with someone you deeply care about. Driving past an old place you used to live at. When your favorite childhood food at the grocery store is no longer found on the shelf. When old songs don't bring you comfort anymore, instead radiating a certain nostalgia that's too unbearable. It's the little things that creep their way into your being: things that might not be substantial enough for you to cry, but enough for you to feel a little more dead inside.

I lost those who never showed up in my corner the way I did for them.

After I sat with my emotions and acknowledged the heavy truth, my mindset shifted from one of grief and loss to embracing new beginnings with gratitude.

And I will find all the parts of me society tried to bury.

I've already found many.

Our existence is meant to be savored and guided by soulful intuition. Living is to be unapologetically reckless, mindless, and unstable. Within the depths of my being rests an unwavering sense of comfort that relies on indulging the full spectrum of emotion because the same ones which drown a soul also gift it life. I desire character and unpredictability and a fearless adoration for melancholy. Consistency has never appealed to me, and each time I find myself settling in the cracks of stagnancy, the embers within my heart refuse to settle for anything less than a wildfire of intensity. A sense of stillness is nothing more than nightmare fuel. I need to feel it all. I need it to consume me.

No longer hiding
who you are at your core
is the most freeing feeling
in the world.

It's completely and unequivocally here for the taking: your life and the all-consuming flicker of passion. You can decide your trajectory at any time and change direction. You can wake up one morning and listen to your bones as they whisper with certainty what you deserve. Allow your intuition free rein and follow its calling. The right path will be discovered. All you need to do is pay attention.

I am forever accepting my darkness and diving into the depths of my subconscious, forever living in that space between harshness and acceptance. This soul of mine seeks fresh air and salt water as much as it craves to be crushed and rebirthed. A human being's complexity is to be many things, all of which are contradictory.

I hope you unlearn their projections.
I hope you discern which advice to take and disregard.
I hope you become everything you always knew you were.
I hope you are at peace with the soul that you are.

People always ponder how one could live in isolation but never what it takes to get there. From the outside, it seems the one existing on the outskirts of reality is bitter, lonely, grappling with an understanding of peace. Maybe the general consensus gathers an individual's aversion to society. But what is not seen are the years trying to come to terms with betrayal and investing time and energy toward false hopes and intentions. What others don't see are the chances given that keep blowing up in their face or the promises broken to oneself about how this time will be different only to be scolded again. They picture a spiteful, lonely silhouette that keeps to themselves, but never the monsters who sucked the life out of them.

Once I let them misunderstand me and create a collection of self-serving stories to justify their behavior toward me, I was able to find peace.

You can paint me in any shade you choose.
But I'll always know the grace with which I treated you.

No amount of bullshit can change the truth.

Understand that I've been through too much alone. In the times I had been struggling, I still held space for those who needed me. And I wouldn't take that back for anything. But because I had opened my arms, I had unconsciously created an open invitation for energy leeches who tried taking advantage of my emotional generosity. Going through hell and back with insincere people in your orbit changes you. You soon realize the true meaning of loneliness. However, despite this, a corner of your soul that is even more empathetic is born as the rose-colored glasses shatter across the floor. Moving on from the wrong people becomes effortless. Boundaries become a necessity. I would say I'm still the same person, just acquainted with life experience. But I found out in the end who really cared and who didn't. And this freedom I now have is priceless.

It's not that
I don't care about others
or that I'm stuck up.
I've just learned
to stop giving my warmth
to those who take it and run.

There is consolation in knowing I was the last one standing. I am at peace knowing I tried everything I could. I find comfort in the longing, the waiting, the fighting until the very end because I do not have any regrets lingering above my head. I held on with everything I had until there was nothing left, my spirit remaining content with no questions unanswered. I will never forget what we built. These memories will forever rest within the abyss of my subconscious to revisit, to remind me what we shared was real and it exists. Maybe we were meant to cross paths and not walk it together to the end. And I am coming to terms with the realization this does not make us any less special. For a moment in time, we were immersed in something uniquely ours: a constellation of magnetic fragments so impassioned, so irreplicable, so magical. A home of memories made to last a lifetime in another dimension.

You won't find
this heart of mine twice,
and I promise darling,
one day, that thought
will keep you up at night.

Your spiritual progression will be a target for those who want the easy way back in. Remember who left and how they did. Remember the way you were treated without romanticizing the manipulation. Remember every night spent second-guessing the kindness of your spirit and the extent of disrespect you tolerated. Nobody holds the right to evoke that sense of internal discomfort again. Absolutely nobody.

My motivation is unwavering.
I embody resilience on a monumental level.
Emotional vulnerability is my greatest gift.
My authenticity will not be sacrificed for anything.

When you care about someone, their wins become yours to celebrate together. Surround yourself with those who share the inspiration and don't view your accomplishments as competition.

I will tell people how I feel and wear my heart on my sleeve even if it backfires, even if it's a one-way street because I could not live with myself if I withheld my true feelings for someone I cared about. I couldn't part ways without them knowing just how deeply they had touched my heart.

Vulnerability will always be my default.
I'll never be ashamed of that.

They looked at me with crowd mentality, eyes rolled with pointed fingers keeping them company while insinuating the existence of my crazy.

With a grin on my face, I blew them a kiss and started dancing, looking up with gratitude at the sky because I could finally be myself without caring.

The dedication to stand in my truth and be who I say I am has been affirmed by the countless times I could have followed the route expected of me and didn't. I remained loyal to my morals during the most crucial of moments. I chose consistency and solidity over popularity. I prioritized integrity in spite of rejection. But ask me if it was worth the cost, and I would say yes, a million times over. I have loved and lost. I have been excluded from spaces I believed accepted me unconditionally. However, my conscience is as light as a feather because I have one thing in my corner they don't. I can look at myself in the mirror.

Some personalities have been shaped by others, both consciously and subconsciously, without any valid reason aside from an aversion to difference.

Some find hesitancy in living authentically because with each quirk, each dissimilarity in opinion, each streak of resistance, they were punished, ridiculed, and excluded. Unlearning the imprinted expectations of others is not for the faint-hearted, and there may likely be moments when one doesn't believe it is possible.

But this journey will remind you of your resilience and the importance of sticking by your values as a person. A newfound feeling of freedom shall find a home within your bones once the limiting beliefs which once controlled you disintegrate into the earth. Slowly, but surely, alignment between your spirit and flesh will occur.

The internal confliction will weaken gradually as you distinguish your thoughts and feelings from theirs.

Day by day, your self-identity will strengthen, leaving less room for uncertainty and more room for exploration, acceptance, and harmony.

Suffering can become comfortable if you're not careful, and misery can turn into your drug of choice. And it's an addictive place to be when you realize how safe it can make you feel. But once you have a taste of peace, life will take on a whole new meaning. Pain is only good as fuel, for reflection, or redirection. Feeling it constantly is a reality we're capable of changing.

Focus on where you're going and how deserved it is after fighting for as long as you did.

Sometimes,
a second chance
closes the door
between you
and the person
you thought
was the one.
Sometimes
it's a necessary
heartbreak.
Sometimes,
a lesson sinks in
for the final time
when another round
of damage is done.

It can hurt when you demonstrate patience and warmth toward someone you care about and they don't reciprocate it or take it for granted.

And it's difficult for it not to feel personal.

But just know that some personalities allow others' true colors to bleed out quicker. So be thankful you got out before they completely tainted you.

Your kindness actually saved you.

Right now
I'm trusting
I'm growing
into the person
I'm meant to be.

Choices become blessings
when you see what they
saved you from.

Darling, why would you even want to be anyone else after witnessing your own strength? *They haven't been what you've been through. They don't know the things you do.* You're telling me you'd prefer to be someone else without knowing a single fact about their true self instead of this wickedly unstoppable forcefield of a human being with unlocked potential waiting to explode?

I refuse to hide anymore.
I refuse to alter my energy in any capacity
to make others comfortable.
If my sheer existence is unsettling, deal with it.
I am in my own lane, always,
so your judgments aren't my problem.
I will be too loud, too outspoken, too much of everything.
I have so much to offer and so much to learn.
I have finally found comfort in being seen.
No longer will I shrink to appease anybody.

The people who believe in Karma
don't claim to be perfect
or think they are faultless.

They believe in it because
they have experienced it first-hand
and know it's not something
to be fucked with.

There is an unstoppable feeling that arises from releasing the baggage of expectation to be a certain way.

Put it down.

Your shoulders don't need to be heavy from their projection.

What they say about you is a reflection of them.

Take solace in the ideal that time softens the most jagged of edges. In hindsight, many of us are left thinking about what once was and reminiscing the positive memories. And although this is equally dangerous in its own right and can invite the temptation of overlooking destructive patterns, such a premise brings comfort that people change, grow, and evolve and can reconnect and build upon a clean slate contrary to how they once drifted apart. Distance reveals what is important. Solitude either heightens or blurs feelings and shines a light on our priorities and what is worth holding onto. Separation may occur as a permanent or temporary lesson. But I do know that nothing can withstand the velocity of fate. The Universe will do everything in its power to facilitate reunion. There is no forgetting and no moving on until the ones who are meant to be together find their way back to each other.

I really believed we were meant for something more.

With you, I felt a connection that I couldn't completely express in words.

But I just feel there was more to the story with you: an unknown in the corner of your soul. A hesitance to get too close. A wild streak of avoidance. Maybe someone you were still hung up on in the distance. It's unfortunate because after meeting you, you were the only one I wanted from then on. The imprints in my heart before you began fading away and clearing space. I was willing to move past the past and start building this new foundation.

But all I can say is what a shame. It's a shame the possibility of us wasn't enough for you to feel the same.

My capacity to love deeply is not reliant on reciprocity. My emotional honesty, vulnerability, and unwavering understanding is a gift which radiates rarity in a world where the consensus is an aversion to caring.

Everyone's replaceable? See, that's the thing. Some people just aren't. And it's a realization that only comes to light after the novelty of a new interaction wears off. And that doesn't mean you're putting them on a pedestal or clinging to a toxic ideal. And it certainly doesn't mean life doesn't or cannot go on after them. But there is something about some people we meet that is so incredibly special to us and by devaluing them we also devalue what we had. You may meet a person that just has something so unique about them: the way they are, the way their minds work. The way they see the world. And it doesn't mean you won't find other amazing people whom you get along with. But there could just be that one person who touches your soul on a molecular level. Their combination of traits were compatible with yours – they made you feel at home. It's okay to admit that some people are irreplaceable.

They made their choice. You don't need to hold it against them because time will tell. Time will tell whether it was the right one. Time will decide how deep their regret resides. And time will reveal relief if it calls for it. You did all you could. You wore your heart on your sleeve, and they decided it wasn't enough. But in most cases, the backlash of a decision takes years to sink in. Once they realize truly genuine people are few and far between, reality will hit them like a ton of bricks. But don't wait on that. You are who you are – don't let anybody dim your light.

When you have a heart that loves as deeply as mine does, you cannot lose. Not indefinitely. Yes, I will be subject to more heartbreak. Yes, I've fallen for those I felt took a piece of me with them. And yes, I'll continue to openly welcome and let go of people over the years like we all do. But loss will never be permanently ingrained in me. I will find beauty in everything around me. I will create connections with others that are enriching and fulfilling. I will always find a way to find what is lost in another form. When you have a love like mine, the world is limitless. The opportunities for gratitude are infinite. I'll never weather the storm alone. There's too much to be grateful for in this world.

Those you'd never think would want to see you sink will jump in the boat filling with water with those who loathe you to finish it faster. Sometimes your enemies are waiting for an opportunity to tear you down behind the crowd to avoid accountability before using their life raft.

Remember, the hateful and weak need a team.

I need you to retain that same energy and distance you comfortably did when I was struggling. I need you to remember all the times I was there for you in your darkest hours and how you turned a blind eye to my world crumbling. I urge you to own your decision and lack of compassion and remain seated from a distance. I need you to understand I will never allow those who made me feel insignificant a seat at this table now that I have found my feet. I promise, I will never allow you back in. I do not hold space for the insincere. I do not have time for opportunists. My discernment has sharpened, and my conscience is clear. You chose detachment with confidence before everything turned on its head. Stick to your decision. I don't want anything you're offering now.

I refuse to let a breach of trust permanently change me. You showed me what you were. And that has nothing to do with me. I might tread with caution for the near future, but there are hearts that deserve and will reciprocate this openness I bring. I won't deny myself a worthy connection because of your dishonesty.

You'll either be the villain in someone else's story for standing up for yourself – or a fool in yours if you don't.

Pick your poison.

The reward for sacrifices made to nourish your growth will become more and more evident as the years go on. At the beginning of it all, you will be on an even playing field with those around you who don't do the work. But with each distraction skipped to focus on your goals, each early morning or late-night session and burst of dedication, the gap begins to get larger. One day, you will be in a completely different place than those who never started. One day, you will stop to appreciate the view and understand every time you chose yourself, it was never in vain. One day, it will finally sink in where you ended up because you chose to put your goals into action and believe in the vision.

When people used to leave,
it used to tear me apart
completely.

Now it's an "I told you so"
that dances around in my mind
and a warmth inside my chest
whispering,
"But you'll always have me."

I say praise
and light a candle
for younger me
who held the power to get us
where we needed to be.

The strength
of your shoulders
will never be forgotten.

Until the very end,
you will be loved
and honored.

Self-awareness and acceptance will grant you peace beyond your wildest dreams. Neither of us can be everything. We each have our individual strengths and weaknesses, and acknowledging this reality is the moment you will finally be free. You can continuously improve in certain areas. You can accomplish goals you set your mind to within reason. But it shouldn't be the end of the world if you try with all your might and nothing changes. Think about how many talents and gifts you possess, and not necessarily exclusively in the realm of art and creation: your capacity for compassion, your ability to offer advice as unique as each sunset, the enthusiasm with which you embrace your emotions and inspire others to feel the same. Your aura is special. Your energy is inimitable. You can't be everything to everyone, but you can cherish everything within yourself.

You're getting up every day and making the effort to be better than who you were yesterday. You're confronting your flaws, your shortfalls, your reactions to circumstances out of your control and implementing steps to ensure your actions are more considerate toward yourself and others. You're in the midst of reclaiming your power. You are working on becoming the best version of yourself. This path will lead you somewhere great.

I lost the desire to be understood.
I just want my soul to feel comfortable in this flesh.

That's it.

Being open and wearing my heart on my sleeve might have led to many misunderstandings and an abundance of suffering, but it reassured me that not even the harshest of circumstances could turn me cold. And that blessing alone is worth its weight in gold.

Maybe that delay was your saving grace. Maybe your plans were laced with elements leading you to a dire fate. Maybe the inconvenience you were subjected to was a detour in disguise ensuring your protection. Be grateful for the road congestion on your way home, the extra time taken to complete your order, the unexpected distraction, the obstacle that encouraged another path to be chosen. Everything is working in your favor, and you don't even know it. Our blessings are not always visible to us. And that is also part of their beauty.

I've always loved a little too deeply, a little too passionately.
But how can I call that a weakness when memories with lovers
have embers of their own that burn inside me for eternity?

Here's the thing about people who love hard:

They're always the winners in the end.

Regardless of the lows life throws at them, they can just as easily bounce back into a state of fulfilment because their ability to feel deeply allows them to appreciate the smallest of blessings.

They might be seen as emotional, overbearing, intense, too much to handle, but only by those who aren't in tune with their own emotions and see it as a burden. But it's an absolute blessing to have someone in touch with their softer side by your side.

Emotion is a gift that shouldn't be diluted in any capacity.

I am just trying to be better than I was yesterday. I am focusing on living, healing, and thriving. I have distanced myself from anything that doesn't align with my vision. I honor my intuition. I express gratitude for my blessings and my lessons. I move forward with unburdened shoulders and self-assurance because everything that once affected me no longer leaves a dent. I owe it to my soul to be comfortable in this existence.

Somewhere down the road,
the reason for my anguish
will make itself known.

Until then, I hold onto hope.

I promise I could not give less of a fuck toward those who have repeatedly stabbed me in the back.

Now I'm cold? I'm insensitive? I'm whatever take you want to spin on it when it's convenient for you to deny accountability.

My entire life, I have always been a beacon of warmth to absolutely everyone, to the ones who have now turned on me. I would radiate generosity to those who didn't deserve an ounce of it. And over the years, it drained me completely. But now I am very selective about who sees this side of me. Even more so, for those who experience it.

So I will take on the chin every insult you want to throw at me. I'll take it all on in a heartbeat, even if everyone believes your lies, for a life of freedom far away from your hypocrisy.

I've distanced myself
from mostly everyone
and everything.

I became fed up
with the drama,
the bullshit, half-assed
relationships, and
insincere connections.

All of my energy is
being protected internally
so I can give back
to the very few in my life
who mean the world to me.

Solitude has gifted me with perspective, peace, and healing.
Strong boundaries have ensured my emotional protection.
I have experienced too much heartache not to be selective.

Prepare to be the villain in their story for finally standing up for yourself. Be prepared for those who exploited your kindness to change the narrative to suit them. The tables have finally turned. Now you stand tall. You will not be walked over anymore.

Just you wait.

Wait until they label
your self-love as narcissism.

Wait until they brand
your confidence as arrogance.

Wait until they try tearing down
your self-esteem while preaching
ideals of inner beauty.

Wait until they project everything
they said they'd never be
all because they can't stand to see
a human being unlearning
everything they're still stuck in.

No matter how often I find myself caught up in the madness and tragedy that is to be found in life, I always make the time to count my blessings and be thankful to be alive.

You need to believe better days are on the horizon. You need to hold onto the faith that you are growing stronger each and every moment despite your ability to recognize it. And it won't be until you're faced with the challenges that once turned your world upside down that you can acknowledge how far you've come because those situations no longer startle your bones. You are on a new path leading you toward the life that is meant for your spirit: one that is pain-free, filled with abundance, blessings, and freedom.

When you go against the grain in any capacity, you are guaranteed to ruffle feathers and make people uncomfortable. It takes immense strength to pave your own way, knowing full well you will be misunderstood and ostracized. It's so very simple to say what people want to hear, to blend within the crowd, to turn the volume down. When you stand your ground and embrace your authenticity, less souls may be in your corner, but at least you retain your integrity.

You can love yourself and make questionable choices. You can love yourself and make mistake after mistake. You can love yourself and willingly choose something that could hurt you. Loving yourself doesn't make you exempt from being human and messing things up. Self-love doesn't mean you're immune from self-destruction. Allow yourself leniency to try new things and screw them up anyway. None of it has to do with how much you value yourself because going back to old habits is in our nature, and they take time to break.

Distance means nothing when the love is genuine. Our worlds are sometimes met with a busyness that pulls us away from those once regularly in our spheres, maybe for long periods. But that closeness is always evident when reconnecting. It's like you never parted to begin with. Just because someone is living their life and tending to their obligations, it doesn't erase a real relationship. No amount of distance, whether physical or emotional, can permanently come between those who are meant to be in each other's lives.

You were the last one
who touched this body
before I broke open,
before these goosebumps
transformed into mountains.
You were the last one
to glance into my soul
before roses flourished
in the earths of my irises.
You were the one
to witness the final chapter
before I finally grew
into the person
I could never be with you.

You can be forgiving without being naive. You can choose both peace and strong boundaries. You can forgive and forget, or you can remember the ones who betrayed your trust and promise to never let them in again. You are entitled to put your foot down when your generosity is being taken for granted. You do not owe anybody a consistently calm demeanour with the expectation you will tolerate mistreatment. Your kindness does not equal an absence of strength. Retaliation to abuse doesn't necessarily make you an unhealed person. Your worth isn't determined by how many people you allow to wipe the floor with you. Discern the moments to stand your ground or walk away. There is no rule book for approaching every situation. Give yourself leniency to adjust accordingly.

Don't feel bad for finally standing your ground when the ones who treated you like dirt come back around. Remember their behavior toward you when you were down. Remember, they would continue to walk all over you if you didn't take a stand. Don't ever forget how they left you, how they felt no hesitation in watching you suffer. Just because they've switched up now, it doesn't discount their neglect when you needed help. It doesn't erase every single second of agony you endured while they were living their life with no fucks given if you continued to.

I never once felt it was wrong to have such a capacity to feel until I saw just how many were willing to use it against me.

In the span of just a few short years, everything you endorsed with certainty can be turned on its head. The beliefs you strongly upheld will be questioned. You will be tested. You will be left heartbroken to such a degree where cynicism begins to creep in. You mustn't let it.

Take what you need, and grow in the direction most suited to your purpose. Survival is a priority, and sticking by your values is important. Don't let the world take them from you. Never allow people that don't truly know you dictate how you spend your time on this earth. Don't let circumstance turn you into someone you're not. Remind yourself of the person you are and who you wish to be. This journey is yours. Awe-inspiring experiences are waiting to be lived.

I'm grateful
my path
is being cleared
for the right things,
the right people,
the right opportunities.

I will not grieve
what is not meant for me.
I will open the door
and smile big, hands
signalling the exit,
sipping on this
martini of dreams.

Your defiance
against their opinions
solidified the day
you prioritized
your purpose.

Sometimes isolation is self-preservation.

I hope you know that courage looks like many things and does not always equate to an absence of fear. Courage is wearing your heart on your sleeve after being hurt repeatedly. Courage is choosing honesty and prioritizing your spirit's integrity. Disagreeing with widely held opinions is courage, as is being self-aware and admitting when you are wrong while promising to continue learning. Feeling nervousness or doubt or overthinking into oblivion and still jumping in the deep end is courageous, and so is allowing your soul's passion to run free in spite of your body's hesitance to be seen. There are many circumstances where you could have hidden from the world but stepped into the forefront that you should be proud of. There will be many moments to come when you will be tested, and I hope you remember all the obstacles you have overcome and channel your power to keep moving forward.

You reach a stage
where you can
no longer break,
and the only
choice left is
to rise with
grace.

I am consumed by the dreams I desire for a reason.
I am compelled to chase them for a greater intention.
Simultaneously honing and following my intuition,
I will fight until my vision is brought to fruition.

If you're someone who has never felt right in this world, I want you on my team. If you've never felt your energy mesh with theirs, I want you on my team. If you're a soul full of everything society says you shouldn't be, I want you beside me.

I don't hold it against you for not returning the same energy I gave you. I would never withdraw the support I provided, the nights I was by your side with empathy and advice. I am eternally grateful for the memories made together. But in the end, I had to choose myself. I couldn't keep allowing you to diminish my worth. I couldn't continue pouring my spirit into a connection that ended up not being genuine. I couldn't continue to betray myself in your presence.

To the one I can't go a day without thinking about...

I had to finally choose myself.

I needed to leave behind whatever we were or could have been to follow my soul's calling. I no longer have it in me to wait around for the one who is unsure or holds just enough curiosity to keep me on the backburner of possibility. I need someone who is so unequivocally certain of their feelings toward me that I feel safe in this intensity. I was never so assured until I met you, but this energy cannot sit here, flaming and lonely. I'm so grateful we found each other at one of the lowest parts of each other's lives. Thank you for everything. These tears have grieved the potential I saw in us. But it's time for me to move on and find someone who knows without a doubt I'm the one they want.

The depths of my love,
passion, and loyalty
are unmatched.

And it takes me longer
than most to move on.

But once I do,
when that switch
is flipped,
I guarantee
you've forever
lost me.

Sometimes you need to forgive them again and again until your heart finally has enough.

Sometimes moving on at the first chance leaves you with questions unanswered and less closure than if you were to let them carry on and disappoint you for a final time.

Don't be hard on yourself for wanting to see the best in them, for being patient. They chose to take advantage of that fact and it has nothing to do with you and everything to do with them.

At least in the end, you can take solace knowing the what ifs don't exist because you tried it all and nothing changed.

I've lived a life
of complete
and utter madness
and I'm thankful
for all of it.

A person's kindness does not diminish when creating and enforcing boundaries and refusing to tolerate unfair behavior. Even the most patient, forgiving, and understanding people have their limits and they are entitled to make the necessary changes to protect their well-being.

Take me as I am or get lost.

I sincerely mean that.

My entire existence up until late has been one of acceptance toward others, even when it would not be reciprocated.

Accept me for my messes, my imperfections, those days when my mouth is too big and I say something I shouldn't.

Just like everyone else, I'm not perfect. I'm sick of trying to keep up this image of perfection to be accepted. Those who truly know me love me regardless because they know I'm a good person. I have a heart of gold, and I'll confidently say that. The thing is, most of my life I was always around the wrong people who couldn't see what I had to offer or they did and wanted to keep me at their level.

That all ends now. It's been over for a while, but from this moment on, it shall be solidified. Let this be my written pledge of this fresh new start: the one that says I refuse to shrink myself to appease those who'd find any reason to leave me out in the cold.

Never underestimate the temptation of external validation.
Many abandon themselves just to feel something.
The same ones who accept you for who you aren't
will not hesitate to exercise a ruthless discard
at any opportunity you dare step out of line
and challenge ideals guarded with all their might.

Nurture your soul's light in spite of popularity.
If you don't, you risk losing everything.

You are under no obligation to bring with you the ones who were distant and uninterested in your journey until your hard work came to fruition. Your selectiveness is your protection.

Some people are waiting to reap the rewards of proximity without providing an ounce of support and encouragement because they take your carefree nature for granted.

The ones who deserve to be by your side during the highs are the ones who felt proud to stand by yours during the fight.

If fate brings us together again,
I will count my blessings.

And if fate keeps us apart,
I shall be equally grateful.

Most will say they
cherish imperfections but
run at the first sight of them.

I want to meet someone
who actually means it
when they say that because
there isn't a person I've ever left
or looked at differently for showing
themselves to be broken.

In fact, it made me love them
even more.

There are some people
I still love from afar.
I'm hoping for them to do well,
to achieve everything they wish.
I've drifted from the world.
I've found solace in silence.
But my heart is still cheering
for those warm souls who
showed me nothing
but kindness.

I'm forgiving
toward the right people
for the right reasons.

I'm not a cold soul
who is intolerant of remorse.

But I've come to find
there are two kinds of people:
the ones who are genuinely
sorry for the way they treated you –
and the ones who always saw
you as an option and are only back
to test your limits.

Don't think I don't know
the difference.

You can choose to ignore the criticism or channel it to drive you further forward. You can choose to be complacent or make it part of your mission for them to eat their words. Don't get it twisted, you're still doing this for you. You are simply tapping into the negativity and using it as fuel.

I'm no longer
overly harsh
toward this soul
that lives within.
I used to beat
myself up for
everything.

What I put
my spirit through
was pure cruelty.
I didn't have to
treat myself
how they treated me.

But I know better now.

It's time for forgiving.
It's time for nourishing.

You've been through enough already.
Don't turn against yourself.
Your soul deserves rest.

One day I told myself,
let them see your madness.

Do it.

The mad ones
will love you back.

Your self-love journey will show you the ones who are genuinely happy to see you loving the skin you're in and the ones who had more to gain by watching you suffer in silence.

People like to
mistake kindness
for weakness
until they are
on their knees
begging for
forgiveness.

Everything
comes full circle.

Once I decided to hold the door open for people who wanted to walk away without feeling compelled to explain why it was a mistake, my life changed. I know my worth, which is why I no longer fight for others to. But the truth is that to some people, I won't ever be seen as a loss. And that's not to say I don't have the incredible qualities I remind myself of every day. It means everybody needs different things. Not everyone appreciates what I will. And vice versa. Every single soul is healing from their own traumas which come with their own complexities that I will probably never grasp in their entirety. All I know is what I bring to the table, and my patience, willingness to stick by others, and unwavering devotion has healed and is capable of healing the most bruised of hearts. But I won't hold it against anyone wanting to leave anymore. I don't need to welcome them back with open arms, but I can let go of the expectation to hold anyone accountable other than myself.

Your greatest power lies in self-awareness. When you know who you are at your core, nothing and nobody can throw you off course. Acknowledge your shortfalls. Admit your flaws. Embrace everything you are and everything you're not. Find contentment within imperfection. Don't seek to be everything at once. You are enough.

I am a wonderful collection
of everything that made me,
everything that broke me,
and everything in between
that keeps me going.

Don't ever apologize
for being honest about how you feel,
for telling and showing people
just how much you cherish them.

Because we never know when the
last time we spend with someone will be,
your heart and soul deserve the closure
of knowing they knew what you felt
for them was real.

If your soul truly loved them,
they knew it too.

Energy exchange is a divine thing.

I finally reached a point where I no longer sought to be understood. Truthfully, the desire had wilted. I had spent the first half of my life chasing validation and acceptance, but over the years something internally gradually shifted until the world took on a different appearance. I began prioritizing inner peace. I held onto everything that nourished my spirit. I spoke less to those who didn't appreciate my voice. I let my soul take the lead – its passion dictated my every move with unapologetic ferocity. I felt less lonely being alone than around those who didn't hear me. I no longer searched for understanding. I had found serenity within.

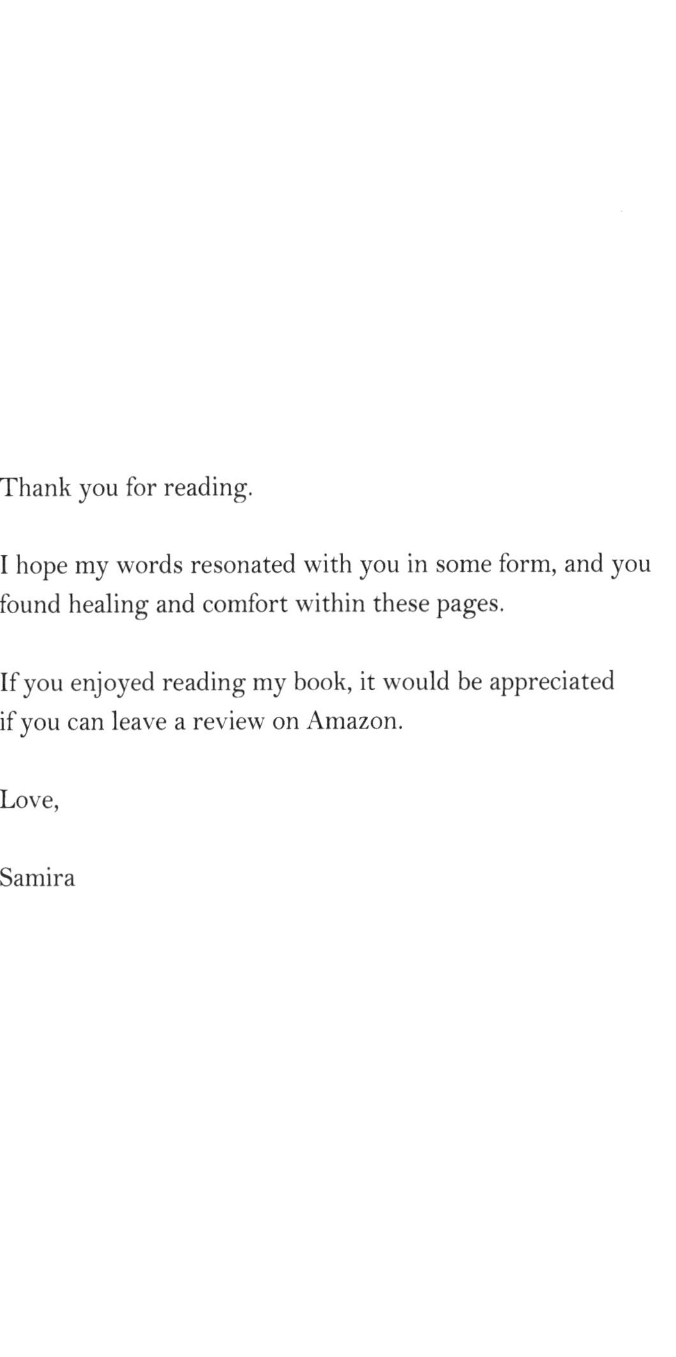

Thank you for reading.

I hope my words resonated with you in some form, and you found healing and comfort within these pages.

If you enjoyed reading my book, it would be appreciated if you can leave a review on Amazon.

Love,

Samira

Made in United States
Troutdale, OR
08/28/2024

22388840R00086